The Little Muslim Book of Mawlid

A Green Fig Book
Illustrated by Bihar Abdulaziz

Book design by CHY

CHY Illustration & Design

DEAR PROUD MUSLIM KID

We hope you enjoy this picture book! The drawings in this book are artistic depictions of events and not how they were in reality, because we don't know how they truly looked.

NAME: ....

Dear Parents & Educators

God, The Exalted, said in the Qur'ān: ﴿ وَمَا أَرْسَلْنَاكَ إِلَّا رَحْمَةً لِلْعَالَمِينَ ﴾
This verse means that God sent Prophet Muḥammad as a mercy for the ones who follow him, among the humans and jinn.

We praise Allāh and thank Him for sending Prophet Muḥammad ﷺ, the Prophet of Mercy, to guide the people, and for making us among his followers. His birth is a great blessing because he showed the truth and exposed the falsehood. He saved the people, bringing them out of the darkness of blasphemy into the light of belief.

The birth of Prophet Muḥammad ﷺ is a great and joyous occasion filled with merits and blessings. Celebrating his birth - the Mawlid - is an honorable practice that shows our love for the Prophet and our devotion to him, and this inspires others to do the same. This commemoration started in the early part of the 7th Hijri century. This was an innovation-that is-a new practice, that was initiated by *Al-Mudhaffar*, the glorious and generous King of Erbil, in Iraqi Kurdistan. The scholars of both the East and the West judged this innovation as a good, rewardable practice that honors the Prophet. Since that time, Muslims all over the world have been celebrating the *Mawlid*, united in their love for the Prophet ﷺ.

Green Fig is pleased to present to our young readers *The Little Muslim Book of Mawlid* recounting the story of the birth of the Prophet ﷺ and some of the amazing events that occurred around it. When hearing this story, children's love of our Prophet ﷺ, the best of all the creations, is increased and they are reminded to praise Allāh and thank Him again and again for blessing us with the Prophet of mercy ﷺ.

We love to hear from you at info@gogreenfig.com

Green Fig Team

More than 1400 years ago, a young,
good woman from the clan of Bani
Zuhrah named Aminah, the daughter
of Wahb, lived in Makkah, the best city
on earth. She married 'Abdullah, the
son of 'Abdul–Muttalib from the tribe
of Quraysh, the most honorable tribe
of the Arabs.

Not long after they married, Aminah became pregnant. Then 'Abdullah left Makkah to go to al-Madinah for trading. He died during that trip and Aminah became a widow at a young age.

Aminah was patient with this hardship.

In the early stages of her pregnancy, while she was between wakefulness and sleep, she heard someone giving her the good news that she had conceived the master of this nation and its prophet.

Aminah said that from this, her pregnancy was confirmed to her and it was a Monday.

Amazing things happened to Aminah during her pregnancy and delivery, indicating the high status of the child she was carrying.

One time in her dreams, Aminah saw a tree with shining stars on it. One of the stars was the brightest of all. As she was looking at that star, it fell into her lap.

The tree in the dream symbolized
Prophet Ibraheem, the forefather
of Prophet Muhammad. The shining
stars symbolized the prophets among
Prophet Ibraheem's offspring.

The brightest star that fell on her
lap symbolized Prophet Muhammad,
to whom she would give birth.

Other special things happened with Aminah during her pregnancy. She said she did not feel the burden of pregnancy that most women feel.

Birds used to come to her and stay close to her.

When she would go to
the well to bring water,
the water would rise up
from the well to her.

Towards the end of Aminah's pregnancy, a big event happened in Makkah for which the year was named "The Year of the Elephant."

A Christian king named Abrahah came from Yemen with a huge army to destroy the Kaabah.

He brought with him a very big and
strong elephant named Mahmood
with twelve other elephants.
Abrahah's army advanced until
they reached the borders of
Makkah. Suddenly, the elephants
refused to move forward.

Whenever Mahmood was directed to advance towards the Kaabah, he would sit and not budge. But when he was directed backwards towards Yemen, he ran in that direction.

God sent black birds from the direction of the sea. Each one of them carried three stones, one in the beak and one in each talon.

Each stone was bigger than a lentil but smaller than a chickpea and on it was written the name of Abrahah's soldier it was going to hit. The stone would enter the head and exit from the bottom of that person. All of Abrahah's army died from these stones.

By this, the Kaabah was protected from being destroyed by that evil king without any fighting.

Fifty days passed from the incident of Abrahah and the Elephant. It was the night of the 12th of Rabiʿ al-Awwal ربيع الاول, the third month of the lunar calendar. Aminah was alone in the house when she felt she was going to give birth to her baby.

She was distressed because no one was there with her. Then she looked to the corner of the house, and saw four tall women, beautiful and fragrant, wearing white clothes. She asked them, "Who are you?" One of them answered, "I am Maryam, the daughter of ʿImran. And the one on your left is Sarah, the wife of Ibraheem, and the one behind you is Hajar, the mother of Ismaʿeel, and the one in front of you is Asiyah, the daughter of Muzahim.
These were great pious women that lived before Aminah.

Aminah was very happy to see them. They reassured her and helped her with her delivery.

الأشهر القمرية

المحرم	صفر	ربيع الأول	ربيع الآخر

جمادى الأولى	جمادى الآخرة	رجب	شعبان

رمضان	شوال	ذو القعدة	ذو الحجة

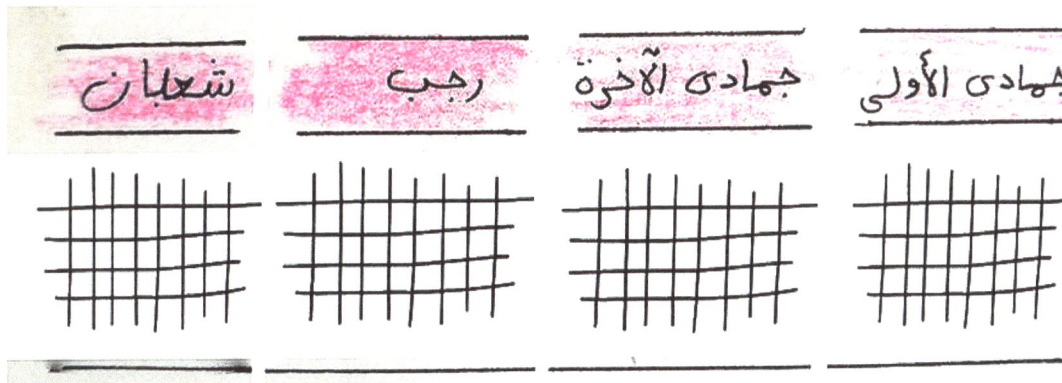

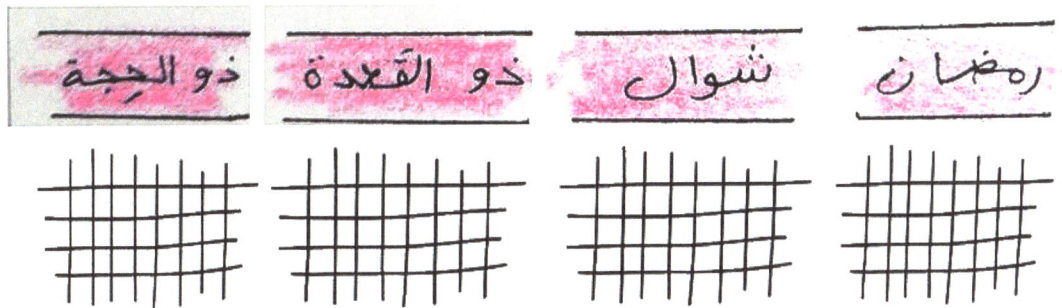

Aminah said that she did not experience what other women usually experience with childbirth, but that she sweated a lot and it smelled like musk.

Then a big white bird passed its wing on
Aminah's belly and said,
"Descend O Prophet of Allāh".

The most beautiful baby was born!

Aminah said that she saw a light that came out with the baby which was so strong that it reached the castles of Busra, a faraway city in Syria.

The baby boy was born clean, resting on his hands, looking up, with his eyes open and naturally lined.

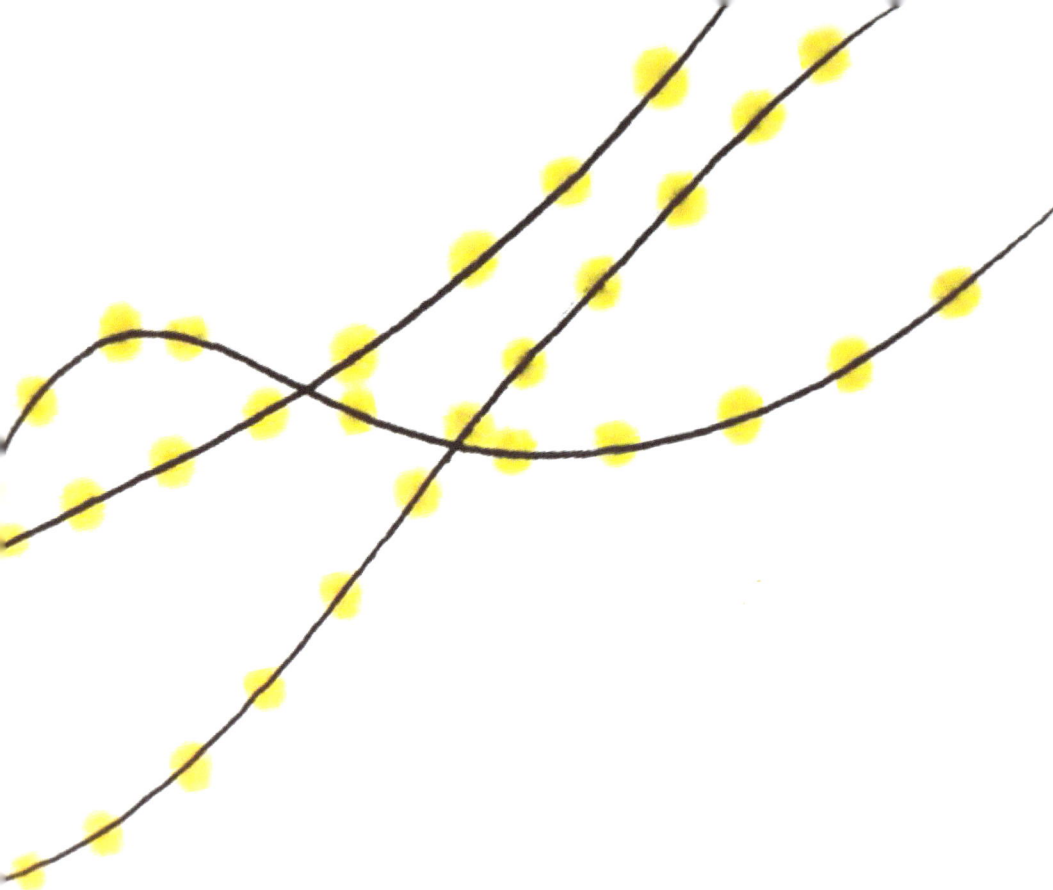

The best of
the creation was born
in Makkah,
on Monday,
the 12th of Rabiʿ al-Awwal
in the Year of the Elephant.

Monday 12

Many more amazing things happened during this blessed night, the night of the birth of our Prophet Muhammad.

The huge fire of the Majus, who were blasphemers who worshipped fire, was extinguished. It had been burning continuously for one thousand years in Persia and on that night it died out. This was a sign of the truthfulness of the message of our Prophet to worship God alone.

Also that night, the palace of their arrogant king, Kisra, shook and fourteen balconies fell from it. This was a sign that only 14 more Persian kings would rule that area before the Muslims would take it.

This is exactly what happened, during the time of Caliph 'Uthman.

Abdul-Muttalib was very happy
with the birth of his grandchild.

He called the boy Muhammad,
which means: " the one praised
by many for his many good
attributes. "

Muhammad grew up in Makkah
and even before he received the
revelation was known by all the
people as As-Sadiq, Al-Ameen—the
Truthful, the Trustworthy. He was
patient and brave.

He received the revelation of prophethood when he was 40 years old, and began calling the people to worship the one true God, the Creator of everything. He immigrated to al-Madinah when he was 53 years old, and lived there 10 years. He died in al-Madinah and was buried there.

He was the best of the prophets and messengers and the one with the most miracles. His message spread across the world and today more than a billion people follow his path on the true religion, Islam.

Hundreds of years after Prophet Muhammad's death, al-Mudhaffar, the king of Erbil, a beautiful city in Iraqi Kurdistan, held a grand celebration thanking Allah for His great gift, the birth of the final Prophet, who led the people from darkness to the light of Islam.

Large structures with wooden domes were built for this occasion from the old citadel to the city center. The story of the birth of the Prophet was told as well as speeches reminding the people to work for the Hereafter. Thousands of portions of food including meat and dessert were set out for the people to eat.

Every year, Muslims including Muslim scholars would come from faraway cities to attend this celebration.

Since that time, in the month of
Rabiʿ al-Awwal, Muslims all over the world
follow this good practice of celebrating the
Prophet's birth.

**We call this occasion
the Mawlid.**

They recite Qur'an, praise the Prophet,
and tell the story of his birth.

To show their joy, they decorate the mosques and the streets. They walk in parades. They distribute food and sweets.

Muslim Kids are very happy
during Mawlid time.
They participate in Mawlid
celebrations and in joyous
activities in schools.

They learn about the
Prophet's life and their love
for the Prophet becomes
stronger.

We love our Prophet
Muhammad.
We thank God for this
great blessing: the birth of
the best of the creation,

Muhammad,

مُحَمَّد

صلّى الله عليه وسلّم.

Encourage your child to memorize:

The Prophet said:

﴿ إِنَّمَا أَنَا رَحْمَةٌ مُهْدَاةٌ ﴾

Which means:
Indeed, I am a mercy given as a gift to you.

Proud
Muslim
Kids

The Proud Muslim Kids series by Green Fig is designed to engagingly teach youngsters basic concepts of Islam in a way that speaks to their hearts and minds. Each book in the series is crafted by a staff of qualified educators, writers, illustrators, parents and children. Not only is the Proud Muslim Kids series designed to supplement the early childhood and elementary Islamic curriculum, it is a great addition to any school or home library. Covering a wide variety of topics such as the Five Pillars of Islam, Islamic culture, and Islamic history, parents and children will return to these books and enjoy them together time and time again.

About The Illustrator

Bihar Abdulaziz is a high school student in Canada. Drawing and illustrating are some of her favorite hobbies. She also enjoys working and spending time with children.

Book design by CHY

CHY Illustration & Design